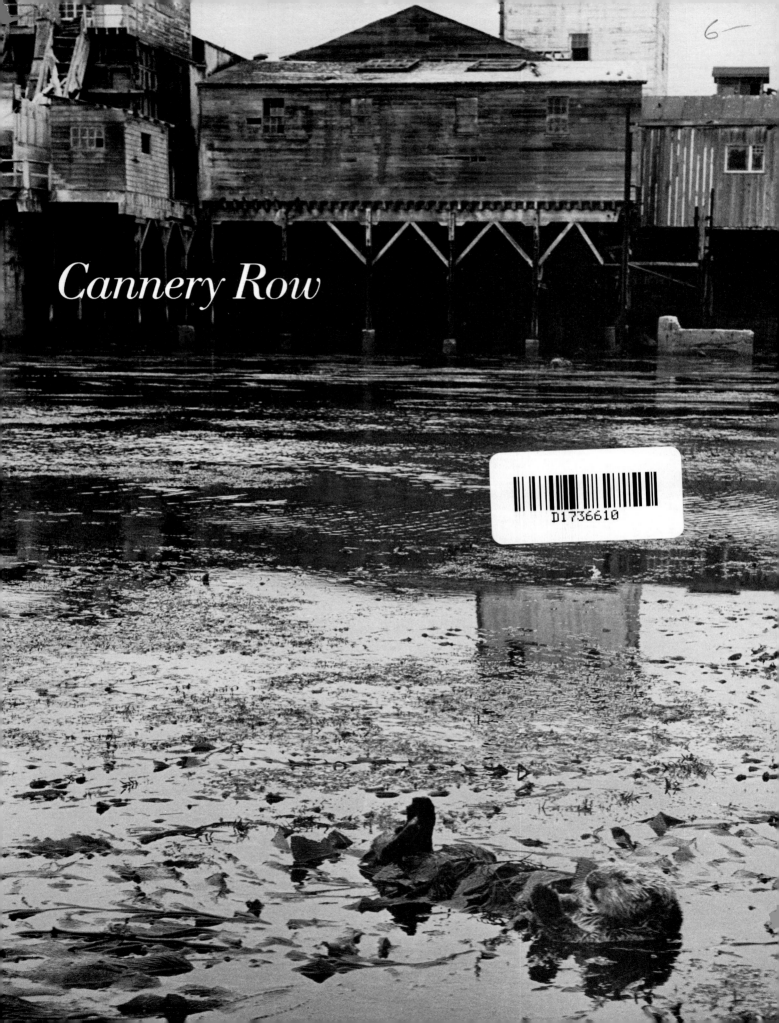

Cannery Row

Published by COWPER HOUSE
P.O. Box 32, Pacific Grove, CA 93950
All Rights Reserved
ISBN 0-917223-00-4

Printed in the United States of America

The photographs in this book have been selected from three permanent exhibits hanging in the Monterey Conference Center, the Monterey Cannery on Cannery Row and the John Steinbeck Library, Salinas, California.

A portion of the proceeds from the sale of this book will be used to fund the John Steinbeck Library and the Monterey Library Fund.

A John Steinbeck Companion Book

CANNERY ROW

A · Time · To · Remember

Photography & Text
by Tom Weber

Foreword
by John Gross, Director
John Steinbeck Library

ORENDA ▧ UNITY PRESS

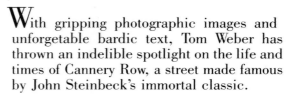

Foreword

With gripping photographic images and unforgetable bardic text, Tom Weber has thrown an indelible spotlight on the life and times of Cannery Row, a street made famous by John Steinbeck's immortal classic.

Just as Steinbeck wrote about an era long gone, so did the author-photographer of this book draw his words and images from the past, painting a vivid, graphic and empathetic backdrop for the Cannery Row story.

It was a different life in a different time that Steinbeck celebrated. His genius captured a special piece of Americana that will live as long as people read.

'Cannery Row' symbolizes an era that will never come again. Everything is gone, the sardines, the characters, old fishermen, cannery workers, canneries, Doc and the 'boys' and Dora and the 'girls.'

But when you read Steinbeck's Cannery Row and let your eyes and fancies linger on the pages of this book, "A Time to Remember," an enchanting story of yesterday jumps out at you in full life.

You will be touched by the 'magic' of Cannery Row as seen through the eyes of Tom Weber. The author of this book has given the street a new dimension and preserved for us in a most fitting fashion, the legend of Steinbeck and the street he wrote about, a street that will survive forever in the world of living literature.

JOHN GROSS, DIRECTOR
John Steinbeck Library

Prologue

Here they are,
images of old Monterey . . .

splinters and reflections from the past,
canneries washed in piebald grays
by moody suns and harried rains,
the wood marred soft by flailing sands,
clawed raw by talons of wild sea water
and aged by cold winds
that shook the rafters loose from shivering.

I ran to hold these images
before they left no trace at all.
But you can't grab much from running time . . .
perhaps the tune of a wistful song
or stories threadbare from retelling
and always the cold black numbers
that lock the feats and failures of yesterday
in tombstone graphs.
These are for the catching.

But not the shrieking shafts of cannery whistles
bouncing off the black-night fog
calling cannery workers:
"To work, to work,
the fleet is in.
It's better to work than sleep."

That sound will not come again.
Nor will the sudden splash of lemon lights
from clapboard windows in humble homes
where cannery workers yawned themselves awake
and ran to snatch
'another day, another pay,'
a crust of morning bread,
the moan of evening love . . .
and all the living in between.

You could not capture these,
nor the sighs and grunts
and sounds of mingled moods
and profanity in a dozen tongues.

Who knows where they all came from,
Portugal, Italy, China, Spain . . .?
Who knows what all they talked about
while they cleaned and canned
and boiled sardines?

One day the whistles didn't blow.
"The fish are gone," the canner said
and hungry workers
turned their hopes to other trades
in other places
and took away the warmth
of their simple people noise.

All gone, now,
and the old fishermen with calloused hands
from pulling line and mending nets . . .
and the creaking sighs of restless wood
in the angry blast of squalling nights . . .
and the ever haggling seagulls
dragging strings of fish gut from the bay.
Going, too, are the few who remember.

Here then, are these images
from the time of other men
who came and built and fished the waters
and thought their dream would be "forever."

Here is their "forever" now:
the rotting planks and doorless doors
and window sashes with glassless holes
that sucked in torrents of winter rain
and called each fog like a reckless lover.

And in the bay, the concrete piers
that once held up a stage of life,
now are marker shrines
where canneries stood.

TOM WEBER
Monterey, California

Who knows where they all came from
to catch and can and pack sardines?

They lived in humble homes,
tied their dreams
to the tail of a silver fish . . .

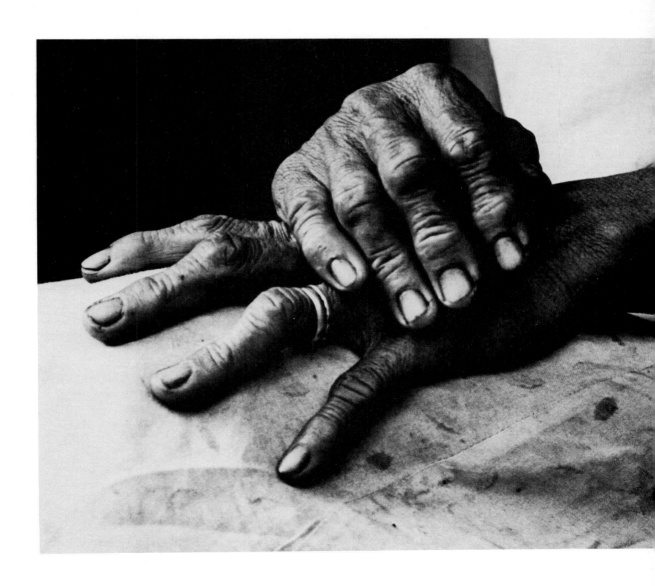

One day the seiners hoisted empty net.
The silver fish were all used up . . .

cannery whistles died of rust . . .

Fishermen rigged their boats
for other fish . . .

to troll the waters
or drag the bottom

and hunt whatever the sea would give . . .

They are hunting still . . .

Fog-wet silence
brushed the sardine street
in shades of scaling gray . . .

In the bay,
a few reflections from the past

where otters
dozed
in cozy quilts
of tangled kelp

while I ran to catch these images
before they left no trace at all . . .

A rusty shovel, a little brine,

nets to raise and dock the catch

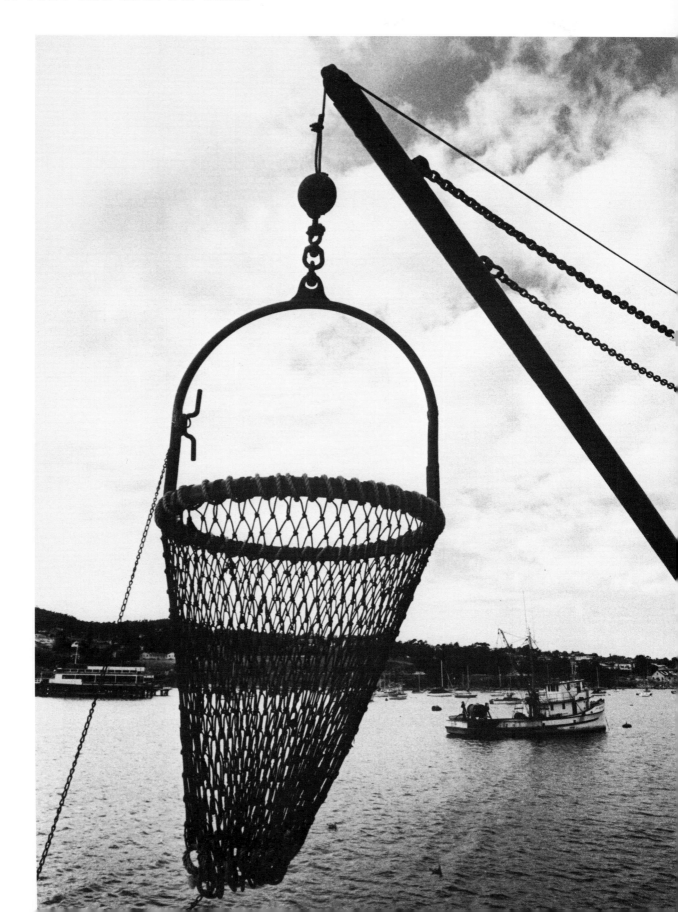

A sardine dump for the cannery fleet

A flimsy shed to butcher the fish

And out of the way for none to see,
there were acres of abalone shells,
another plunder from the bay . . .

There were hotel rooms for fun and pain
that reeked of fish and human sweat,

Chinese murals on a wall,

the anchor of a sailing ship.

And tunnels of smells
of ripe sea life
that swallowed the moan
of the lonely street.

With the fisherfolk gone,
a new cast of actors came on stage.
They were dreamers and pimps,
poets and whores,
moochers and con men,
buffoons and bums . . .

*They made their homes
in the festering hulks.*

They looked out at the bay through the sashless eyes of yesterday's "forever."

*They drank their booze in Rickett's lab
and splattered their dreams on the floor.*

*They slept
in shambles
of rubble . . .*

and mountains of tin.

*This was
Steinbeck time . . .*

The time of bordellos, beans
and homespun hooch
and Wing Chong's grocery store

A time of the ebbing tide,
a quiet, brooding time . . .

*Down in the bay,
the restless birds
recalled the feast
of better years.*

*The cormorant sat
in mourning black . . .*

Seals barked lazy to the sky.

As quietly as they came,
the actors left the stage.
The desolate street
took a turn for the worse.
In the squalling storms
of a winter's night
you could hear the retching moans
of the dying hulks.

*Gale winds took
what the tides forgot . . .*

Man and fire did the rest.

. . . and in the bay.
the concrete piers
that once held up a stage of life,
now are marker shrines
where canneries stood.

Epilogue

The play is over.
The curtain falls.
The images are gone.
But just across a page in time
a new show comes to life . . .

It's Curtain Call!
The stage is set. The props are new.
A ballet of 'golden' tourist lights flash on Cannery Row.
A new cast of actors take their places
and listen for their cues . . .

CANNERY ROW

About the Author

Tom Weber, author, investigative reporter and veteran photojournalist is a native of New York's 'Hell's Kitchen.' He has been carrying a camera and chasing stories since he was 18 years old.
` The scope of his reportage for metropolitan newspapers and magazines has touched on every stratum of society. He has interviewed presidents, prime ministers, 'terrorists' and hookers. He is a specialist in geo-politics with strong emphasis on the Third World.

Weber's work as a foreign correspondent has taken him around the world nine times. He has lived with headhunters, photographed his own ambush in the South Pacific and eaten camel meat in Uzbekistan. He also worked as a commercial fisherman and stevedore on the San Francisco waterfront.

He maintains his studio and headquarters on Cannery Row where he has been documenting the 'street' since the Steinbeck era.

Remembering Joe

Over the years, I interviewed several hundred fishermen, cannery workers and cannery owners. Except for my written notes, they are mostly past recall. But there were a few I never forgot. One of them was "Joe."

I was talking with the owner of a cannery when an old man shuffled into the office and stood staring at me.

"Here's just the man you should talk to," the canner said. "Joe has been around here from the beginning of time. Go on, Joe, tell him how old you are . . ."

"I'm 92," Joe said,
  eyes surprised
  like he heard his age
  for the first time.
His words were quiet
  like Monterey fog.
He was thin as a trolling spar,
  arms hung taut
  as trolling lines,
  with a leaden weight
  of wasted years
  in each hand.
Harsh winds, burning sun
  and smoldering dreams
  charred his face.
But his fingers were still nimble
  for mending nets:
"I go down to the bay every day
  to make sure the boats are still there."
The canner tapped his forehead:
  "Joe was one of my best fishermen,
  lost his son in the war.
  Been a little off ever since.
  Sometimes he sits down there on the dock
    and talks to a seagull."
"Sometimes I talk to a seagull," Joe said.